# PEACEFUL POETRY TO LOVE YOUR SOCIETAL CONSCIENCENESS

## Edited
## By

## Ann McCall

ISBN: 0-7596-7963-0 (ebook)
ISBN: 0-7596-7964-9 (Paperback)

This book is printed on acid free paper.

The publication of this book was funded by **Lisa Rhodes Creations Inc.**
http://www.lisarhodescreations.com

**Cover Art**: Pelicans Bathing photo by Lisa Rhodes

1stBooks - rev. 10/15/02

# FORWARD:

America how can we restore you?  This seems to be the question facing Americans and the world today, after September 11, 2001 when the World Trade Center Twin Towers exploded in flames after being attacked by terrorist hijackers flying commuter planes loaded with human beings, used as ammunition to perpetuate violence and hatred; then the third plane flew into the Pentagon killing more innocent lives.  Why has ruthlessness and aggression shown its evil face? How ironic that in the time of need, we the entire human spectrum of design, hue, creed and color have proved that we are capable of helping each other irregardless of what makes us unique from each other; hatred is extinguished by the power of the human spirit in unifying us all in a time of great need and tragedy. This horrific act of terror proved that there is more love within each of us then hate...we as a human race have a chance to make it on this planet together.......

# ACKNOWLEDGMENTS

*These poems first appeared in the following publications:*

**Working Class Revolt** ("Killing Machine," "Corner Jive," "ON and ON")
**AIM** ("For Amadou Diallo"AKA "SLAUGHTERED")
**pirate radio** ("American Nativity With Tragic Possabilities")
**New & Letters**. April, 1999. Vol. 45, #3. p. 11.  ("41 bullets")
**Left Curve**, No. 24, Spring 2000. Oakland, CA. ("The Bronx Street Crime Unit Bags A Suspect")
**STREETS** ("Out of the drunk tank")
**The Reach of Song** ("To Amadou Diallo")
**SOVEREIGN GOLD** ("Police lines: patrolling the perimeter")
**Music of Found Summers** ("Between Here and There")

# FLIGHT: A TESTIMONY OF SEPTEMBER 11, 2001
(Dedicated to those who jumped from the Twin Towers to their deaths)


Nostradamus Prophecies:

**Century 10, Quatrain 72:**

*The year 1999 seven months*
*From the sky will come the great King of Terror.*
*To resuscitate the great king of the Mongols.*
*Before and after , Mars reigns by good luck.*

**Century 6, Quatrain 97:**

*At forty-five degrees the sky will burn,*
*Fire to approach the great new city;*
*In an instant a great scattered flame will leap up,*
*When one will want to demand proof of the Normans.*


I wish it were

the metamorphisizing of stars
        instead of The sky exploding-
Human neurons igniting like a firecracker-

1000's of desperate fingers clutching phone handles,
a last minute stock quote, crunching of numbers and more lists
of things to do…

a friends husbands dejavu is remembering sitting
at his desk with his fingers cradling the phone,

the reverberating opening bell,
a feeling of his body now flying like a hunched over fetus in an

invisible womb, the computer screen just a familiar

distant world,

now all that is emblematic are his signature pens, business

letter head, a pair of Nine West shoes left staggered on a pile of debris,
celluloid photos of death throwing out

its anchors, its extremities seen washing up like sea drift on a beach,
after jutting its
canopy like wings across the World Trade Center roofs,

         the horizon line is an
infinitesimal arrow reaching across the world: China, Portugal,
                                             Japan,
                                        Russia,
                                         Canada,
                                       Asia,
                               Kuwait,
                               Australia,
                         India,
                       Iraq,
                    Saudi Arabia,
                      Iran,
                     Israel,
                  Pakistan,
              Palestine,
                 Syria,
                  Assyria,
                   Lebanon,
                       The United Kingdom,
                         Uzbekistan,
                           Afghanistan,
                              Africa,
                               Europe,
                              South America
                               North America…
            separating our two human hemispheres,
            splitting the poor and rich, sick and well,

   the numbing silence of those who leapt out of the burning World
Trade Center
Twin Towers ejecting
through space, time, atmosphere, galaxies exploding,

   Oh, God a cell is forming into a zygote somewhere inside a test tube,

those shocking thoughts… and questions of those watching
the 9 A. M. news,

Oh, Christ they are leaping or being forced out of windows;

      can they still dream while

being awake?  Is the Maharishi bowing?

Black smoke billowed until astonished eyes

      saw the color purple and the sky fell like confetti

as the white horses drag the coffins
down Church Street, the asbestos moon covers

the night like a chalky blanket
spreading out over ghostly embraces, holding each other tight,
photographs-

      hung like

grief around the city, the cell phones miraculous ringing gave birth
to hope, which
slowly pieced families back together,

each fragmented thought connecting like earth

worms to warmth, blood donations, are you O positive, does anyone
know if

my pet is ok?..................Does God know today is
my grandmothers birthday?

The last minute anxieties - Oh, cold winter

sun, I want your heat to burn the brain of those who sent this hellish
explosion to my

window.

I want to fly like a pigeon to those bread crumbs scattered in
                Central Park by
the woman who is homeless and who holds a winning lottery ticket
and the Nobel-

Peace Prize in the palm of her hand.

Will the wind hold me tight against the iron cold

mask keeping my thoughts contained like the ebony shaped bones
framing my frozen
eyes in an angry gaze?

Is it better to die this way then to be afraid, to obliviate the end

by recognizing the idiocy of time clamping my veins?  The yogi
can do it and so can I
remembering I am a lint fragment, a molecule of fire; I extinguish fire
when I die,

death isn't the end,-

my arms still carry me in the wind, …I am a kite with a very long

unflammable tail, a red helium balloon that doesn't want to be found

by just anyone, I-

escape my captors, an open hatch appears, my eyes travel inside,
a wonderful flight,
many colors are there, worlds reunited are one,

                        the bees are eating honey in their

hives, the water is warm over my eyes-
opening then closing immersed in this love filling up inside
of me until…

                I am full.
**By Lisa Rhodes**

x

*For Ghandi, For Nelson Mandela, For World Peace and Healing, For Amadou Diallo, For the Families and Victims of September 11, 2001, For the Homeless, For the Future Generations*

"Our bodies are tired, and our feet are somewhat sore, but today as I stand before you and think back over that great march, I can say as Sister Pollard said, a seventy-year-old Negro woman who lived in this community during the bus boycott and one day she was asked while walking if she wanted a ride and when she answered, "No," the person said, "Well, aren't you tired?" And with her ungrammatical profundity, she said, "My feets is tired, but my soul is rested."

Dr. Martin Luther King Jr. (from his speech "Our God Is Marching On!)

# TABLE OF CONTENTS

## Peace


We passed their graves:
The dead men there,
Winners or losers,
Did not care.

In the dark
They could not see
Who had gained
The victory

**By Langston Hughes**

## On The Occasion Of Her Son's Funeral

*Dedication: To Doris Boskey whose son, Gary Gidone Busch, was killed by the police.*

The woman stood flattened,
    a paper doll,
held up by others
    more dimensional.
Her broken son,
    her heart's obsession,
Torn, stripped, severed,
    ripped away by bullet fire.
Savagely she cradles his coffin,
    clinging to rage to keep breathing.
Life has asked too much.

**By Linda G. Peltz, Ph.D.**

# 41 Bullets

In an America mesmerized
by fantasies of soaring stock
and of heroic police saving lives,
bursting villains,
41 bullets punctuated the heartlessness
of days questing for profits,
41 bullets punctured the flesh of Amadou Diallo,
scattered his soul on the steps of his Bronx home,
red-splashed the respect shown to immigrants,
blacks,
workers,
life
so the eyeballs of America had to see,
just as cops' other bullets have torn flesh and scattered souls for
decades,
displaying a "just-us" soon forgotten
by the media of the bottom line
but never forgotten by the cops and their guns.


**By Samuel R. Friedman**

## Paean to Tepatepec

Shivering cops,
bodies bare to Mexican winds, to everybody's eyes,
while the people of Tepatepec defend justice
letting freedom sing
while two million prisoners suffered
from policemen's lies
and businessmen's needs
in the colossus to the north,
once land of the free.


**By Samuel R. Friedman**

# If Mumia dies

If Mumia dies
of the spiraling epidemic
of police-mouth lies,
let us turn our minds
to revenge,
thoughts of after the revolution
as well as "how to,"
to thoughts of ex-cops in day-jobs,
night-jobs,
tending the graves
of Mumia's ghosts.


**By Samuel R. Friedman**

## Public Transportation

Herding em' in
too quick,
too fast
like the train
we rode too far,
above ground,
past Harlem
into the Bronx.
Van—
Van something.
Our skin
the only white
too tender,
too juicy.
Dark eyes
staring
wanting to take a bite,
draw a little blood,
make a mess.
Did we taste sweet,
would our meat
tear easily from our bones?
"Go sit by the conductors box
and don't move"
Or would it be tough
to chew
salty
acidic bitter?
"What the fuck were you thinking?"
The cops spoke in unfamiliar unison,
tearing at the zippers of their nylon coats
revealing bullet proof vests
wanting us to see
what danger looks like
up close
before it begins.
"Do you know where you are."
Rhetorical.

"You have no idea where you are
do you
do you?"
The cops in unison again.
Or would our skin
lodge itself between their teeth?
And if so, would they pick it out with
a matchbook edge
a pocket knife,
or would it rot
in the gum pockets
deep holes
where teeth once grew
before the heroin, the crack
the urge to kill
for a single hit?
"God Damit!"
The cops vest stared us down
trying to provoke fear,
trying to provoke tears.
But I smiled at every jab
thinking how cute
they were
protecting,
armed,
under cover.
I kept thinking
about the story
looking down at their shoes,
if we lived
It would be a great story.
"Don't move
do you hear me
don't move"
The smaller cop threatening,
the older cop shaking his head.

My grin growing,
angering the cops
to beat on their vests
and say in unison again
"What the fuck were you thinking."


**By Devorie Franzwa**

# Out of the Drunk Tank

"Slipped,' they said
from two tiers up

came cart
wheeling

down

landed
head first
right outside
my cell

sounded like a watermelon splitting

when his head
hit that
cement
floor

'Just some old
drunk,'

they said."

**By Sheryl L. Nelms**

# The Bronx Street Crime Unit Bags A Suspect

Hard white guys hunting down the perp,
serial rapist, lower than whale shit,
scum of the earth type a guy.  Get a scent,
track the punk to his lair,
teach him a lesson, get decorated, some face time
with the brass, the pols, the fancy, weed & Jack,
a little free pussy.  Life is good.

Street Crime Unit on the prowl.
Urban counter-insurgency cadres,
metro retro green berets, thinking like a veritable
fire breathing, gut-busting, kick ass street machine,
blood streaming in their blue veins,
hair up on their pale necks,
carotid arteries in overdrive,
muscle tense, bulging, laser eyes scoping the avenue,
plain clothes, plain car, ready to rumble,
what it means-WE OWN THE NIGHT!
Heart of the jungle, they spot an African.

LIKE THAT IT GOES DOWN!
1157 Wheeler Avenue, combat zone.
Jittery spook in the doorway, little past midnight,
witching hour, hot flash of badges, spook fidgets,
he is packing, reaches for his heat—
MOMENT HAS COME!
9 millimeter semi-automatic pistols, cleaned, oiled,
safeties released, drawn aimed, squeezed off in one
practiced liquid motion, clip of 16 garlic-tipped cartridges
itching to be emptied—
MACHINE IN ACTION, JACKSON!
POP! POP! POP!
Basra, Racak, West Bank
THUK! THUK! THUK!
Slugs slam into the perp, sheer velocity
keeps him up, he bends, twirls, writhes, pirouettes
in the furious molten melodies of the fusillade
SPOOK CAN DANCE!

Cease fire, perp down, vermin contained,
street cleansed, quality of life protected.
Sleep tight, don't let bedbugs bite.


Swing into damage control mode.
No piece, just a beeper & a wallet,
no record, a peddler, religious.
Not a word from Edward McMellon,
Sean Carroll, Kenneth Boss, Richard Murphy,
just grim white faces, clenched jaws.
Barrister in place, narrative ready.
He is acting strange, he fits the rapist's description
in a generic way.
Ambulatory male spook, 12 to 75 yrs. old.
Despite repeated identifications & orders to this individual
to do certain things, he failed to comply
Detect that tough homey, fuck you attitude.
The reason they are shooting him is because they think he has the gun.
Spook with gun, better safe than sorry, no fags in this
Car full a stand up white guys, Bronx Street Crime Unit, got off
41 shots, 41 shots, 41 shots, new mantra, magic number 41.
19 hits in 41 shots, batting. 487, not a bad average for these
New York Yankees who take no prisoners,
1 to left chest, 5 to left side, 1 to left back, 1 to right arm,
10 to legs & for good measure, 1 to the sole of his foot
maybe so he don't get up and run, ruptures of aorta, spinal cord,
lungs, liver, spleen, kidney, rest of ordnance embedded in the
wall, door & foyer-approximately coffin sized.
Street Crime Unit was here, have guns, will travel,
untouchable. Answer to $64,000 question—
why no witnesses come forward.


The reason they are given this kind of fire power
is to neutralize what they perceive as a threat.
While it may seem to a layman to be excessive, it was
the number required before this man stopped.
This man o man o man is,
was Amadou Diallo, West African known as Ahmed,
immigrant from Guinea, Muslim, prayed to ALLAHU AKBAR!
5 times daily, 22 years-old, single, read books on Islam,
Christianity, computer science, rooted for Chicago Bulls,
spoke softly with a slight stutter, street seller of videos

taking home $20 for his 10 hour days
outside the storefront on
14th Street
New York City
Manhattan
3rd World.
Object of what law enforcement officials

(speaking on condition of anonymity) call
contagious fire, when your partners see you shooting
& think your life is in danger they open up, discharge,
let loose, join in a kind of contagion,
like target practice, armed riot, turkey shoot,
ducks in a barrel, gang bang, all of which
troubles the Prince of New York who urges calm,
let's be level-headed, no jumping to conclusions,
describes how this thin blue line is taught
restraint, cultural awareness, cultural sensitivity,
that there are more spooks offing each other
as a percentage than there are police officers doing it.
Broken record drones on.

Old faces/new faces/young faces/worn out faces/
worker faces/housewife faces/vender faces/loco faces
homeless faces/Boricua faces/ thinking that could a been me faces/
handful a pale faces/mostly Black faces/all furious faces.

Incandescent outrage, familiar slogans,
customary cadence of chants,
previous placards adjusted for the latest name,
fill in the blanks, sounds of marching feet on the cold, cracked
pavement of Wheeler Avenue in the South Bronx winter
where water now boils in the air.  Ululating wails
in the mosque, thousands of hands reach to touch the
plain pine box inside of which are mortal remains
of generic would-be defendant, forever neutralized,
his 19 holes plugged with embalming wax, a little heavier
for all the uninvited lead he still hosts.  Old Cadillac hearse
moves slowly, the Harlem Sea all the people parts,
the cortege assumes its position, its columns a great, shimmering
metallic being, headlights unblinking under a leaden sky,
north through the valleys to the great gray river & over it.

The long way home.
Not the route he had in mind.

The folks arrive from Africa to claim their son.
Businessman father, mother in traditional headdress,
a floral pattern. She says, Amadou was from Guinea but now,
Amadou is from the whole world, because the whole world
is sympathizing with us.
Whole world learning how the Bronx Street Crime Unit
bags a suspect.


**By Jon Hillson**

# I can't believe I'm 54

In a night black as the pupils
of a sleeping panther,
everyone is in bed
on the black side of town,
of Chi-town by the lake.
All is still, all is bright.
Doors slam inwards.
Fred Hampton dies.

It is May.  Sultry Mississippi air
seeps through holes in dormitory walls,
bullet holes hosed by cops
just doing their duty.
Students die.

The man my cousin married, and later divorced.
went down to Carolina in the seventies,
postured at a rally,
chanting "Death to the Klan."
Jim's body warm
under a Carolina sky.

Long after I left Ann Arbor,
I learned the true name of Robbie,
a friend from SDS.
He had not been born a Meeropol.
He had seen his mom and dad
taken
by men in suits and badges,
taken, tried, murdered
by those who defend "life, liberty.
and the pursuit…"
against Jews and Commies named Rosenberg.

Somehow, I have lived to be 54.
I have not seen my doors smashed inwards.
My dorms and homes have remained unbulleted.
My demonstrations met tear gas and bully clubs,

not rifles.
My skull has remained inviolate,
even though Los Angeles police used the skull of a colleague,
Geoffrey Symcox, as an anvil,
even though managers have offered teens
hard cash to beat me,
even though I defied the mob
to transform the Teamsters.
I am fifty four.
I have not yet been
disappeared.


**By Samuel R. Friedman**

## Ginsberg Is Dead

of my own stupidity
got arrested during
National Poetry Month for
Operating Under the Influence
the bar was 3 blocks from my house,
anyway, I called the coffeehouse
so someone would bail me out

overhearing whom I had just called
the cops figured out my name
and immediately rode my ass about drugs
"there isn't a poet on the planet not into drugs"
"we know your into drugs, and we can go easy on you,
so c'mon tell us, who are the 'other poets'?"

I told him Ginsberg is dead.

**By José Gouveia**

# On and On

"We have over two million people behind bars in America, 70% which are non-violent offenders.  Put in a cage for smoking grass or having a sickness or addiction or because they are political prisoners to a fascist, corporate state."

prisons and people
lock down on a dream
dehumanize what we create
judge man by progress made by law
defeat him when he crawls for belief
torture him if he bleeds
if he becomes educated
complete his knowledge with a shovel
in hand create a monster out of a man
morals and God mean no more
if the rules our made
use them lose them
but belong to the sliding door
it becomes you and me
on and on and on and on
till there ain't room for no more
till the mind gets numb
when the jailhouse gets jammed!


**By Israel Bayer**

## Always Open Season

1.

blood soaked
in the sin of a society
sick with the disease of discrimination
and the denial of its own resident evil:
                                          racism

you were caught
unprotected by your civil rights
under a hailstorm of semi-automatic acid rain
a bullet shower of forty-one drops of death
caused by poisonous Gestapo gases
blowing out the ass-mouth of Rudolph Giuliani

you drowned in the flood of gun-fire
turned it to blood
this plague will persist
until America's hardened heart is broken
by us
and justice
        flows
            forth.

2.

Amadou
Amadou
Amadou
it was you
not your wallet
that posed a threat to them
the wallet was just a convenient cover-up
a white lie            an aryan alibi
for their calculated caucasian craziness
it was you
as in your Black skin
that provoked their paranoia
that led a lynch mob of forty-one bullets

to maraud&mangle your body
it was your Blackness
your dark skin
your ebony frame
that framed you

it could have happened to any of us
who are Black but
it was you
Amadou
and all they saw was your skin
the overseers gaze cast down on the enslaved
you are not the exception
          an isolated incident
your murder is the proof
and our lives testify to this truth
that justice turns her blinded eyes from seeing
that we are not free
we are still a colonized community
tied to the whipping post of the past
slave legacy lingers
like the stench of death
Dred Scott stares forth from your life-less eyes
our lives garner no respect

and so the system moved to the murderer's defense
but to this we scream: DEFIANCE!
we gave up the Sambo smile of submission
a long time ago
when we witnessed Emmit Till's mangled face
and watched his momma cry
something on our insides changed forever that day
we shed our fears
and unmasked our rage
no more running away
no more denying the reality of our oppression
no more making excuses
their insanity was not unacceptable

there is no other explanation
you can't rationalize racism
and it is this craziness

that colors the lens of our lives
and leaves us asking "why?"
and leaves our jaundiced eyes unable to find justice
it is this insanity
that creates the insecurity
that we carry in this country

it is always open season on us
we are walking targets
in occupied territory
a community under siege
with no refuge
no asylum
no amnesty
all we have is ourselves

but this evidence will not be entered into the judicial record
it won't even make the morning news
but it is this evidence on which we stand
and rest our case
of being born the hue of our history
with the birthmark of fate
we bear the brand of those murdered because of our Blackness
a piece of us is buried with them
as we wrestle for some peace
in the coffins of our confinement
their spilled blood is pumping in our veins
for we are one
and we know we are right
no matter how many juries genuflect
to the wishes of white supremacy
we will never give up the fight
We Will Never Give Up The Fight
WE WILL NEVER GIVE UP THE FIGHT
for we know we are right
and we know who the real threats are

3.

the real threats
are they who are deadly
not because of their guns loaded with bullets but

           because of their minds loaded with bigotry
             minds manufactured in fascist factories
              the same factories that created

                    slave ships
                   plantations
              whips, chains and Jim Crow

reservations
scalping
diseased blankets and broken treaties

concentration camps
ovens
showers and the swastika

the opium wars
wage slavery
and the atom bomb

ghettos
barrios
shanty towns and sweatshops

prisons
the death penalty
three strikes and lethal injection

it is they who are the real threats
to society and civilization
it is they who have wreaked havoc on humanity
it is they who are the rapists, robbers and con-men of continents
the serial killers of the century
murderers of the millennium
it is they who are the real threats

it is they who deserve death.


**By Ewuare Osayande**

# Of Course He Had Good Reason

## To Smile

America when will we end the human war?
                    from Allen Ginberg's America


of course he
had good reason
to smile
of

                    course
as he wrapped
trembling wrinkled
ninety-two year old fingers
around his lemonade glass
          and sipped
          and rocked away
on his nashville front porch
chuckles
in his throat and his heart
as he thought about a law and order
          Mississippi son
who shot a nigger in the belly
seven months ago
for stupidly trying to stop
a good ole boy
     from beatin some sense
     into nigger parents
     at one a those
     rabble rouser
     martin lucifer coon rallies
and
of course
about how an all white inquiry
found no reason
          to indict the officer
which prompted him to pleasantly
reminisce

(radio on the wooden deck squawking out
ike at a white house press conference)
about a carte blanche badge wearing
good ole boy
        rapin a nigger gal
        in a monngomery cematarah
and of course
good democratic white people in charge
found no reason
to charge the officer
and about
two other carte blanche


        wearin good ole boys
        who stuck thair lilah white pricks
            intah variouz plazes on a nigger gal
and of course
an all white democratic grand jury
found no reason
to indict the officers
and
of course
he could not help
but reminisce back further
to when good general
nathan bedford forrest helped found the knights
and then ike
brought him back to the present
when he mentioned something
        about the evil god dizhonorin commies

then abstract time
marched across redstained concrete clouds
like an old newsreel about hitler
marching across a movie screen
to silently witness (1993)

in affluent black middle class
prince george's country maryland
archie elliott
shot fourteen times

killed
while his motionless menacingly
unarmed dark skinned male hands
          remained handcuffed
               body crumpled in the front seat
                         of the police cruiser
               still threatening brutality against the police
and of course
whites in charge there
found no reason
to indict the officer
to silently witness in new york (1995)

little honors student
yong xin huang
playing with friends and a bb gun
killed
by a big cop
shot
in the back of the head
while he faced and struck the officer
and of course
a mostly white democratic grand jury
found no reason
to indict the officer
to silently witness (1999)

mentally disturbed harmless
hasidic jew gidone busch
shot to death
          for menacingly holding a hammer
          in his harmless hand
          over his thoughts far removed head
          in front of his law abiding house
and of course
a mostly white gentile democratic grand jury
found no reason
to indict the officers
to silently witness (1999)

american dream through hard work
african street vendor

amadou diallo
shot
accidentally
nineteen times
and accidentally shot at
twenty-two times more
while his black body lay
menacingly still
shooting back with red
and of course
a mostly white democratic grand jury
found no reason
to indict the officers
to silently witness (2000)

patrick dorismond
a wrong haitian juvenile become
an adult gainfully employed right
security guard
shot
in the belly dead
because he indignantly and insolently
punched no to drugs
into the face of an unidentified stinging cop
stranger
who asked him for some
and of course
a mostly white democratic grand jury
found no reason
to indict any officer
and of course
only a contemptible unamerican dogooder
like a hillary clinton
or a racist (racial superiority spouting)
like an al sharpton
would find a correlation in all this history
and of course
no old dynamo program
could ever help

a computer graph equations
to show there is definitely

was is and shall be
a correlation in all this history

and then also in 2000
there were still living
mississippi bones fleshed over
withered hate white
propped up in a wheelchair
before a squawking tv
in a mississippi nursing home
trembling wrinkled
ninety year old fingers
wrapped around his coca cola bottle
who reminisced
about a nigger's body back in the fifties
anointed by blood seeping through bandages
lying still in a morgue
reminisced
about carte blanche badges and guns
    and fictional reports
    and loud wails
    and nigger protests
    and chuckles
      in his throat and his heart
as fading blue eyes
contentedly saw
the new york mayor complaining
about certain rabble rousers
and antipolice bias

as the two eyes
slowly and peacefully closed
on the lacrimal new york nigger family
    and greedy newspeople
    and camera contrite policemen
    and the defending new york mayor
    and a read op ed newspaper piece by mark goldblatt
      warning about dangerous dark skinned males
        the police face daily
    and john doe and mary poe new yorkers
who unlike a good ole boy
were just too clever to say nigger

and
would wince at the sight of it on a page
but demand the democratic right for it to be spat
who obviously knew what they were doing
in the new order
clannishly chirping
       about racist al
       and carpetbagger hillary
       and innocent cops
       and tragedies

       and accidents

all that raucous combine
tramping across video
while his final
serene smile thought
was


of that twenty first century
undying mostly white and always democratic grand jury
of john does and mary poes
in new york maryland and elsewhere
in the good and holy u s of a
that defeated the ungood
    ungodlah god dizhonorin evil empah
that found no reason
that finds no reason
that will find no reason
       to indict the officers

and then of course the startled nurse
       standing at the wheelchair
       noticing the dropped coca cola bottle
         seeping brown blood beside one wheel
       feeling the absent pulses
       viewing the closed lids the serene smile
         on the peckered pink face
then saying
to the hysterically sobbing
eighty eight year old girlfriend

aht lees heah went peacefully mizz winifred
   plezant smahl on his face an awl
of course he
had good reason
to smile
of

       course

**By Robert Betts**

# Killing Machine

(about policing agencies in America and around the world)

Dope tied to justice
Police man give your bullets a name
Poor + education = death by circumstance
Modern day lynching
Not guilty newspaper says
Lock down on the grid
Times are a changin'
      that's what the song said
Worlds colliding
Killing machines born and bred
Dressed in blue
      and armed with ignorance
Keeping the beat
      installing the madness
Back on the track
Ultimate deception
Peace keepers with a pistol on hand
Restoring our culture with a shovel
      and a rope     a tree
to hang the innocent for living
to ravage the life from true men.

**By Israel Bayer**

## Corner Jive

The rain is falling hard tonight
Me, the bum, and the prostitute sit out on the curb
Drinking 40's- talking about, well who the hell knows man
Not a thing in common, but everything's the same down hear
Standing on the beat…ducking behind the same ravine
Philosaphazin' the superior motives of our blackened conquest

One ask to for change to buy some booze
"Spare change…spare change…could you help a homeless man out of the rain."
All tattered in the ocean of reality with worn out shoes

Suzy looks for a prospect on the fly
Hangin' round for some blow tonight

I stood there mumbling about to and fro
Spraying words on brick, blue acid tone
Early mourning chills took my senses to hell
Plowing the asphalt exit with rubber soul art

Reacting on the dime- blue light chasing
Them Nazi mother fuckers chased our sorry asses
Down the line, all in due time, hide -n-seek in the hood
The homeless man and me shot out into the night
The heat snuffin' us out like wild savage predators
Back around the houses alley sprint into the street
Flying around a corner ducked into a bar
The bum found a dumpster somewhere behind the joint
Bathroom stall beat hiding in the urinals
The pigs had Suzy, her first date done fled
The police man did his job—
got her down on her knees again

Its mean-n-hard, its the streets, better believe
Poor people down, tired and surviving
All colors pouring out their guts and bleeding.

**By Israel Bayer**

# Facing Adversity

These were the enraged times
In which humanity waged torrid warfare
Against itself.
Against those of different ideals;
Against those of different beliefs;
Against those of different nations;
Against those of different carnals; and
Against those of different skins.

These were the enraged times
In which intimidation and corruption
Stabbed the hearts and
Blinded the minds of others.

But not some.

These were the enraged times
In which individuals of epic compassion
Risked their own lives—
And those of their loved ones—
By assisting those who were in
Great need.

Those who were of a different breed.
One has already done the deed.
Others will follow.

**By Greg Roman**

## Between Here and There

*Berkeley California, for S. in Poulsbo Washington*

Does every afternoon ripen
so irrevocably?  A peach that cannot
contain its juice,
a sun that no shade tree
can tame but that bursts and bursts its skin
until millions of miles of space
cannot stop the rushing.

There was a wind off the bay
that would not be kept still
but lifted everything it could:
undulated old news along the street,
a girl's skyblue skirt, and every hair
along my bare arm rose
until I thought we were all nearly free.

Walking home I missed you,
that quick ache
white glint of the sidewalk
buff of wind,
and suddenly there were a woman's desperate hands
opening against thick glass.
She was shut up

in the backseat of a police car.
Cops standing around
trying not to see her
I wanted to stop say to them
"Release her!  Release her now!"
Wanted to go to the rolled up window
in the way the breeze
cannot hold itself

still, but empties,
empties, snapping and seeking skin, wanted to
match my hands

to hers on the other
side of the glass,

tell her, It's all right.  The air
will move again.  Whatever
craziness is in you on you
in from of this damn culture
you are all right.
But I couldn't, didn't do that,
don't know.

I wanted you
like June air, the way
sunlight surges between
Mayten leaves and presses
clear through.
Skin ache of my bones.
That visceral.  This has been
enough time between

enough of 900 miles thick
enough away from the between of your
hands.  Now is time for arms
around.  For us in the afternoon.  For
your fingers in mine.  For skipping
weeping juice of the day seeping relentless warm
toward dusk.

In the way
the air moves
and bursts open,
the way it cannot hold
itself, I want

you: the way
nothing is free
enough or
close enough,

in the way the woman's desperate
eyes sought me and found me,
a stranger through thick glass,

walking by, the way
her emptying hands pressed
against the glass between us
and silently clamored through.


**By Christina Hutchins**

# The Kibeho Slaughterhouse

For Nelson Mandela

(*Civil War between the Hutu vs Tutsi*)


The Rwandan battle front
drowned into a red sea:
a private shooting gallery
where government troops
massacred children and woman,
dismembered bodies, stomping
over them, leaving their
footprints bloody branding
bare backs, soaking
each victim like a dry—

ice cube burning minds
touched by
naked eyes, blood, big brother.

It is the Killing Season—
a sport in Rwanda—
to massacre
women and children
for the welfare of politics?

"Scapegoat the babies,
people will listen;
There cannot be a cleansing without
the shedding of blood," said the militia.


**By Lisa Rhodes**

## The Abused People

We are the products of abuse, misfortune, abandonment,
and misery.

We live in the ruins of what once was our livelihood.
A system whose ivory towers loom over us like
chess pieces on the verge of landing on the next square
of the board.

A system whose inhabitants are the rulers of the various
territories they survey in the sport of—
buying, spending, selling, dealing, stealing, trading,
robbing, lying, seducting and killing.

Our association to this dilemma is what you call products of a racist society.

Inhabitants look upon us as lower life forms and
treat us in that fashion by beating us to death, and setting
us on fire.
For this is our fate for being part of the human race.

**By Greg Roman**

*Ann McCall*

# His Rights are Yours (remember?)

An Interrogation 1963-
An anonymous back room
One bright light hangs overhead.
An officer, in the background,
Holds handcuffs and a police club.
A gaunt man, in uniform gray,
Sits hunched on a stool.
Tired, black circles
Outline his defeated eyes.

Doesn't the police officer obey the law?

Coerced Confessions-
Prior to the 1966 Supreme Court
decision of *Miranda v. Arizona*,
Some prisoners suffered beatings
At the hands of police officers.
Interrogations continued
Until harassed prisoners
Broke down and
Confessed under duress.

Where was the public defender?

Miranda Upheld in 2000-
On Monday, June 26, 2000
The Supreme Court upheld the
1966 *Miranda* ruling
That prisoners in custody
Have to be advised of
Their "right to remain silent,"
And to have a lawyer present
During questioning.

Why talk without a lawyer present?

A Recommendation for US Citizens
Exercise your constitutional rights.

It keeps the system honest.

**By Cynthia Cavanaugh**

# The Solution

The way to fight against police brutality
is to have them learn some poetry,
but I'm afraid that poetry will make them strong
as it made me, after they have treated me wrong.
It would actually be even worse
if a policeman beats you reciting some verse.
So I say, let's send these animals, these fools
back to the zoo, kindergarten, and then school.


**By Sebastian Lazar**

## Cops

(dedicated to abner louima)


you
of incandescent blue
and flash of gold badge

you have your own tv show now
where you can be found
cbs-ed and nbc-ed
"cops" in all caps
at 7:00 & 11:30 p.m.
eastern standard time
crashing through subsidized doors
cuffing criminals

i should feel safe
your presence so visible

the far-reaching
forever stretching arm
of the law

but lately
i find myself thinking

if i had to choose between parallel streets
you on one
suspicious-looking street-slingers
on the other
i think i would cross
to their side
of the street

big brother says
that you will protect us
from them
but many of us wonder
with increasing concern

and frequency

just who
will protect us
from you?

I
want to know


we
want to know

hospitalized
haitian
hand-cuffed to his hospital-bed
abner louima
wants to know

who
will protect us

from
our
protectors?


**By Felicia Morgenstern**

## Warren in the Rye

Grant goes
I have to tell you Sergeant
that your son Worn
mouthed off
he was really a wise ass
and we had to slap
him around a bit
we found this book on Worn
you might want to watch out
for what he reads
so he don't get alienated
with everyday life


**By Michael Casey**

# Odium Resartum

(on the tragic, 'accidental' police shooting of amadou diallo, new york, 1999)

<pre>
aren't you
being prejudiced     (!)                    (?)
o why (say can) can't YOU (you)
see (see?)
harlem resident      (!)                    (?)
to the well - trained
police eye
a wallet
held (in)
night
really does
look
like a gun            (?)                   (.)
</pre>

**By Robert Betts**

1. *odium resartum means patched up hatred*

## American Nativity With Tragic Possabilities

The people of the world crowded the streets of Seattle
saying, "we are tired of hearing
    'heres a crown for me, and a cross for you.' "
Here come the piggies
    on patrol.
Here come the piggies
    on the dole.
Here come the piggies
    beat us black & blue
The new face,
    of corporate "screw you!"

Through the armor we hear
    "We serve and protect the corporations,
    this is our dream for the future of all nations."
The left hand of Uncle Sam says,
    "We need greater gun control, we must silence the violence."
The right hand of Uncle Sam says,
    "Heres some tear gas, pepper spray and illegal nerve gas."
The left hand of Uncle Sam says,
    "We need greater gun control, we must silence the violence."
The right hand of Uncle Sam says,
    "Take these rubber bullets,
        in your back,
        in your face,
        in your head!
    "Today these bullets are rubber,
    tomorrow they'll be lead!"
The left hand of Uncle Sam says,
    "The people have the power, the right to peaceably assemble."
The right hand of Uncle Sam says,
    "Back to your factory,
        back to your cubicle
        back to the grind!
    Get outta the streets, get off your ass,
        move aside, let this armored police force pass!"

It's open season on freedom of speech.

It's open season on freedom to assemble.
        Guns only preach to knees which tremble,
                still the bullets fly…why?
        There's no place to hide
                Chief Seattles' returning tide,
Its open season to replace non-representational government,
        the streets fill with the brave majority, saying:
                "My name is Native Son,
                        I'm living under the gun,
                been living on the run
                        since my eyes have opened,
                        since I started to think,
                this society is dead,
                        and starting to stink.
                This is not Chaos, this is no riot,
                        we've heard your caste-room explanation
                        but the people just won't buy it.
                We've had enough of your pyramids,
                        one more lie exposed,
                        one more leader deposed,
                with every product we choose
                        not to make or buy."

I won't build your churches, won't build your prisons
                or police sub-stations,
I won't build your highways, your factories,
                your kingdoms, your nations.
I'm a highway sign full of buckshot,
I'm the just deserves Corporate Seattle got,
I'm a pagan lover, hungry and dirty,
I'm the black-clad hand of justice on N30,
I'm Robbin' Hood in hand me downs,
I'm the solidarity which makes the bosses frown.

Civilization is rotting from the top
        I'm nauseous    from the stench,
my baby and I know a way to make it stop,
        hands full of love and a monkey wrench.


**By DA. Martin**

## A Storm For A Hyacinth

This was the concluding month of the Rodney King Trial.
Rodney King, a Black motorist appeared on videotape—
    all over the world, as the Los Angeles Police beat
             him alive.

      The place of this human rights violation
          is where I dance, to all the dances.

           My calling awakened me in a horrendous haste,
           like a fever plaguing my hotel room.
       The air conditioner breezed cool air—
           pumping it like iron and chills run all over
           the furniture.

           I peel my eyes outside a large picture window
       inside the room, to watch con men frantically
           make configurations around a table,
           and flip coins.

           Suddenly one man appears on the roof—
       dressed in all black.
           Another man marches back and forth
           across the roof
           gaining control of my attention.
       He senses my potential for fear.

           I counted the beats during this scene—

           to get my mind organized.

I wondered if the jewelry store across the street
          was being robbed—

           Or was this a serious movie about aliens with secret
           communication techniques:
      a recent science fiction film where the world was taken over
          by aliens with the help of greedy humans, desperate
      for money and an escape, from poverty and the dumb life

of working hard for a living.

Each second seemed to be rehearsed and intricate.
Silent messages flashed across an electronic billboard

advertisement.
I agonized in silence, recollecting voices:
faint memoric memories of Army men I used to know.
This was real, I was not dreaming.

A premonition warning danger
echoed through my mind,
while I straightened the room.


Feeling hungry and frustrated, I leave the hotel,
in my creamy rented convertible—
very suavely driving around
the block, undecided about eating Chinese or Japanese—
and it's 9:00 p.m.  The streets are distilling
after a rain shower.  A living soul was hard to find.

After seeing a convenience store flooded
with people; I pulled over.
The policeman working inside the store
timed the          minutes of each mad phone caller
standing outside.

An employee jumps up from the counter
and plays a sting game.
I take the cowgirl's step: eyes averted cautiously—
as the employee and the policeman
mark my moves, overtly watching me, as I cooked
my pizza two & three times until hot.

Before departing—
after satisfying my hunger temporarily;
I noticed from inside the store, that the glass windows
were large enough to see everything for at least a half-mile.

Four thugs stood in front of the store:
forty year-old gang members—

gruesome geysers from the city's lost cause population,
       rivalries without guts, emasculated—
unshaven, dirty, cold & calculating.

       As I left the store, they spit obscenities at me—
       flicking their tongues.
Carefully, I got into my car and drove—
       three lights, making a left turn—
       onto a boulevard I named:
       Retribution Boulevard.

       Gang members, dressed in baggy
       pants & t-shirts,
       sat close together on a wall—
       overseeing the street.

       Hard grimaces and steely, contented smirks
shot across at me, as I passed by in my car—
       noticing one of their rival gang members,
       kneeling on the bloody sidewalk,
       desperately dragging himself to the curb—
       to beg passersby's:

       *Help me, please help me,*
       I heard him whisper.

       Frightened, I left him,
       rushing to my hotel—
       to phone the police—
       trying to escape the rat poison
       that sets the city's night life flickering like a
       candle,
       violently promising a storm for a Hyacinth.

**By Lisa Rhodes**

# Tent Caterpillars

1

I was no witness, but the redbud was,
the zodiacs of seeding dandelions,
the boughs of black cherry within which
tent caterpillars have begun their weave.

On the road near Hinton he was weaving,
they say, so they pulled him over.  Because
his shoulders were so broad and his skin
the dark and shine of burnished walnut,

they shot him in the face with pepper spray,
smashed him onto the berm.  His face
for them was the color of dirt,
and amidst that gravel they believed
it belonged.  The mud the struggle ground

into their knees was red, like lichens
of rust over medieval armor. When
the epidermis is iron, what a corrupter,
what a betrayal the rain must become.

2

I am no witness.  I was not there.
I sipped some chablis that night,
envied the tulips their garnet-goblet
intensity.  I peeled some shrimp,
grew melancholy over a movie, then

slept alone, relishing the exceptional
injustice of that absence.  Only the tiniest
tail-end of tear gas tore at my eyes
ten years ago at a political rally.
Gravel has never stippled my cheeks.

And words have so little power.  I cannot

48

rub them like cayenne pepper in
an enemy's eyes, stab them like
an ice pick between hated ribs
and watch the blood blow bubbles.

It happened here, below the Armory,
above the Greenbrier River's never-ceasing
grief shushing shallow over slowly eroding
stones.  If I try to imagine justice, allegorize

some body for it, West Virginia in April
comes close to its beauty.  Here,
as along any road, there are shards
of glass to pick up, sharp-edged as
fresh breakage.  "Banal" was Arendt's

word.  "Common," a Southerner
would say, lopping of the word the way
the power companies lop tree limbs.
Common as earthworms rising
to the surface and rotting after

rain.  Even metaphors age
and are replaced.  Tonight I pull
a branch of blooming redbud down:
in the dark it wets my face.
Fizzing pink champagne, it used to be.

Now I see how fragile the twigs are,
and the blossoms are blood-dark breaking
from darker skin.  If you were here with me,
by this road and this river, you too
could bend towards the saplings,

above the susurrus shattered water makes,
you too could hear carnivorous fog,
the worms rustling amidst their own dung,
digesting the new green of April leaves.

**By Jeff Mann**

# A Season Of Blood

Humans with brutality in their eyes,
Gore in their minds,
Anger in their souls,
And fire in their veins—
wage a series of onslaughts against
the innocent,
For reasons that we—
the rational
Will never comprehend.

We must have the means to combat this
Madness from spreading further.
We must have the means to teach
The next generation to get along with
All aspects of humanity, otherwise—
Like the flame of a candle, as a breath of wind,
Hatred will extinguish the glow of humanity
                              For all eternity.

**By Greg Roman**

# The State of New York City Under Mayor Giuliani

Dignity is a heavy price
that racist cops oblige
only to whites.

In America being black—
awards nothing.  America even discriminates
against Africans—
armed purely with, love thy brother
and thine enemies.

The last free thought on Amadou Diallos'
mind was blasted away,
by the rat-a-tat-tat of four
trigger happy suburban cats.

They were part of the elite—
undercover New York City Street Crime Unit
who fired 41 bullets of cowardice
at Amadou after he reached out to hand over
his wallet—
fearing he was being robbed
by four white thugs.

After Amadou dropped dead
to the ground, his wallet fell naked
only then dizzying his killers
into cold blooded reality.

They had assassinated an innocent man—
who was trying to earn a descent living
as a street salesman,
working late into the evening
to save enough money to send
back home to his family in Guinea, Africa.

This is the State of New York City under Mayor Giuliani.


**By Lisa Rhodes**

## October News

*for Diana*

*the cries of those who vanish*
*might take years to get here.*
                    *-Carolyn Forche*


Portland's first heavy rain fall and the fine
print in today's paper announces Amnesty International
will target the U.S. this year.  It is years after
our first arrests, the death of nuns by U.S. hands in El Salvador,
Queenie traveling from South Africa to teach us liberation
songs, after the Gulf War and watching the police swing
clubs at an eighty year old Veteran for Peace, the unsoft
crack of contact.  Last week the news was filled with fear of
Hurricane Georges making his menacing way towards Florida.
Not from news, word trickles in that in Haiti hundreds are
dead or missing, that every river flooded.
Almost six months since your last letter post—
marked Haiti, where you write, the sixth member
of your Peace Corps group fled after a tire flowered punky
with smoke and flames on his porch.  They thought he was CIA.
But this is not Forche's Salvador, you assure me.  Mainly,
your days are quiet.  Puppet shows with children you say look
like posters to sponsor a child, all huge eyes and bellies
dressed up in pink ruffles and one girl constantly stroking
your white skin.  Working with mothers, translating
stories of elders from French you learned after
the assignment to Haiti.  You dance salsa and
send a picture of the river outside your porch,
write of the kitten that is always under foot,
how you read my letters by oil.
In one letter you're baking biscuits in a pot
on the kerosene burner, saying with imagination
anything can become anything else.
In another you name everything on your table:
1 bottle boiled water
3 bottles empty
5 books

1 journal
envelopes
crayons
okra seeds
sunglasses
coral
You have told your village there is a man
who waits.  At this I laugh, remember the last time
we were together.  You, home from Africa
visiting your mother.  Me, in L.A. because Cory, dying,
called for me.  A dinner of fresh pasta, winter tomatoes,
bread kneaded on my mother's butcher block,
red wine in front of the fire.  My dad playing that old
cracking Coltrane record.  The one that makes me weep.
Looking at your photos of Ghana, of the village where you lived,
of you learning to dance, wearing men's traditional dress.
My father offering more wine and you telling about Elmina,
air so cold in the midday sun, your skin prickled like fire
under the history of screaming in all that silence.

Late that night, after the album's scratching close
and the end of wine, we curled in bed,
where we slept together, sometimes, as children.
Your hands rubbing distance from my neck, my head
resting in your lap, you wondering if you could ever live here again,
nesting under a quilt my mother stitched and an occasional
blinding of helicopter floods against the hill.  Listening
to my father's saxophone until even his studio lights went dark.
Sleeping, finally, legs and arms tangled and my cheek
against your breast in the morning's breath of fog
when my mother woke us with the promise of coffee.
Above the desk where I sit writing to you there is a photo of us
sagging into each other, me dressed in black, you in red.
In a few days Cory would be dead and soon after
you would leave the country, again.  Outside
my window the wind is making flags of the chard,
waving their red-veined undersides against the neon
lavender spokes of artichokes gone to flower.
I look for things to save for you, like the day, driving,
when I almost hit the car in front of me as its brakes
screeched to avoid hitting the inflatable toy globe dancing
in the middle of the quiet street, no child in sight,

and the car facing me stopping also, waving us past,
no one willing to nudge its twirling aside.  Each of us
crawling our careful cars, waiting to sight the child who might
dart out any moment, looking or not looking.  I want to say
it was the bright blue on wet asphalt that made us stop, or
the promise of a child, but I can't.  Where are you now?


The tomatoes are ripe outside my window.  Red, and one striped
green and yellow.  The single chair drips the day into the dirt.
It's stopped raining here, the sky is a fragile blue.


**By. J. Keiko Lane**

# August 15, 2000

(Democratic National Convention, Los Angeles)


6:30pm


When was the last time you kissed in public?
Police in riot gear on all sides.
Evening sun low behind buildings, the moon and streetlamps
not yet lit.  Television lights and flash bulbs brighter than stars.
A tilt of chin opens mouths.
The police lower face shields, raise their batons.

Lip to lower lip
the only sound.

-------------


8:15pm


A finger tapping a palm, a tilt of head and eye,
careful.  look. - sharp shooters on rooftops.
Tony holds a worn poster of Mark - the one from
his memorial march.  Fists in the air.  Silent.
Mark's mouth holding the scream he has held for eight years.

-------------


9pm


Backs flat to pavement still holding august sun.
Our bodies outlined in colored chalk.  Flash of a rifle
from the Federal Building rooftop.
When I rise someone is
writing names.  Five years dead
I still expect Steven to rise from the crowd.

-------------

midnight

From this garden I watch the house where Greg lived
before he died.  Moon stretching toward the hill.
I watch until his room lights are dark.
Police helicopters unsteady the air, make strobes of the moon.
Late summer blossoms of lemon and basil push against my face.
I go back to the dictionary. affiliate.  affine.  affinity (in biology: a relationship or
resemblance in structure between species that suggests a common origin.
In chemistry: An attraction or force
between particles that causes them to combine.)

Even now.


**By. J. Keiko Lane**

# When You Have Forgotten That The Holidays Have Died

There have been many hands on this body from the time it was formed.
Most were wanted and invited on with a smile and they stayed as long as they liked.
A few were cold and had committed crimes of unknown origins, and they left me apprehensive.
It would have been Halloween, much like it was almost Independence day last July, but we were caught doing what was expected of us.

That brought on the neutral hands of the police that bought no emotion into play, but they erased any hope of getting away with a real holiday like our older brothers who were fast enough to be successful at creating any holiday.

It was my brother who taught me about Halloween as he left every car a yellow, runny mass, but the police
would be like walking barriers preventing me from having the success my elders had.

It would not be Halloween and I would rest with my face pressed against a fence that I had never noticed before.  Those neutral hands working their way around me, looking for an explanation other than the obvious.

It felt like the dead were searching for reasons to live, reasons that were obvious to me.


**By David Katz**

## Slaughtered


*(For Amadou Diallo)*


New York City, 1999

I am the ghost of Amadou Diallo
watching my body get riveted
with 19 of 41 bullets, pumping into me—
        seeing
the speed of the whiteman's bullets
castrating my blackness,
bold faces hidden by smoking gun barrels—
and a pile of blue-collar policemens' uniforms
neatly folded in the trunk of an unmarked car.

My frightened hand clutches desperately
        at my wallet—
then slowly opens lifeless
        like Christ's outstretched arms
after hearing the blasphemous word shouted
        GUNNNNNNNNNNNNN!
Who can understand the fear of policemen?
Am I the victim and they the perpetrators?
What language do I speak?
What do the other immigrants say?

My door vestibule is where I stood.
A night silence ached
when my face did not glow.
The sidewalks are bloody now;
I was slaughtered like a brown cow.
Allah, help my people now—
please sweet Allah...


**By Lisa Rhodes**

# Lynch Mob

We
Of the unnamed majority
Have found you guilty
For the crimes
You have committed against
Society.

Crimes to which the system
Failed to comply
Due to the public's cry from
Those politically correct upper classmen—
Who follow these
Gutless sayings of how
"One is innocent until proven guilty,"
And that
"The guilty should have a fair trial,"
And all that other bullshit!
Those (the upper classmen)—
Supported this belief
In their upper class ways,
Wearing fancy suits,
Having tons of money,
Living in big houses in the suburbs,
And riding in those stretched limousines.
They held formal parties every night,
And ran their businesses from
Their private offices
While they were continuously
Screwing their big breasted, gold digging
Mistresses.

They cared nothing for us
(The people at large)
Oh sure, they come to the fund raisers
With their teethy smiles
And their (not so large) donations.
And after all that,
They still treat us like dirt.

And it's because of them,
That scum like you
(Richman's puppet)
Are free doing crimes against us—
Over and over again.

No more!
No more will we stand by and hide like—
Frightened school children!
We are taking a stand to protect ourselves
From scum like you
With whatever means necessary!
Therefore,
We sentence you to death
By our own hands.


**By Greg Roman**

*Ann McCall*

## The Outcasts

How did they come to

the conclusion
      to KILL…?

To eradicate the way they were treated as

      outcasts?

Unimaginable thoughts:evil wishes breathed as casual jokes

from the lips of two middle class white honor roll boys—

both served criminal probation charges for prior crimes,—

one boy born from a home where a parent

was honorably discharged from the American military.

Why were their parents unaware of their teenagers' activities?

The boys staged a massacre for Columbine High School from one of their families' garages.

Where crept the polices' fears of catastrophe, vigilance—

the future…

tumults of two well known outcasts previously swept into the limelight

by resonating fervent dances in misconduct: a foreboding calamity.

What consciousness could have engorged the Colorado Police to flinch and dwell—

to heed the awkward cry's trembling from a scared black father whose black son

was verbally warned by the two white boys that he was their next target.

Why did the Colorado Police ignore this black Colorado tax paying residents' cry's for help

by donning a coat of All American Armor?


**By Lisa Rhodes**

# For Chief Gates

He did cherish, pet, and polish hate

Just to terrify L.A.,

Destroying faith and brotherhood

For his own private benefit;

Rather than to serve the common life,

He chose to strike its major bough

And plunge the fruit of gentle hearts

To bruise and rot upon the ground

Of a semi-barren orchard,

Where nothing else now flourishes

But half-clothed skulls

And clotted bludgeons.

**By Steven Sloan**

## Police Lines: Patrolling the Perimeter

I glide into

my white
Mercedized
neighborhood

at will

night or
day

but you
in your Blackness

are caught
in their
gill nets

each time you
Cadillac

through

**By Sheryl L. Nelms**

# The Naive Thief

The father leaves,
For his job—
At the police station,
With his uniform
Necktie in hand:
A whipping stick
To slap his daughters'
bony naked legs.
Her bleached blonde
Hairs singed
at the ends hung over
Her ears that listened to her

Chanting:" Revenge, revenge
Daddy doesn't love me.
He gives me no
Gifts, no money; friends
I have few
But many aching sores
In my heart."
She is the child
Of all the children
And robbed of her childhood
And how so sweet

She is: the heart shaped
Candy that hangs
From her neck,
The gingham doll
That loves to be squeezed,—
A red apple freshly picked
From a tree.
Three women lurk inside
her coat: one fat, one rude,
And one wicked.
Each week she goes

Shopping, lifting jewels

Here and there.
Nobody will know
her motives tucked inside
Her fathers watch that ticks
Slowly like a noose
Around her heart.
She can go into

A dressing room
At one of these cheap
Stores and change her clothing
The way skiers do,
Layering many skeins
Like hot impulses.
When the policemen came
They took her in the back—
Seat of their car.
The metal grate painted
Numbers on her face.
At the police station

They don't care
How naive you are
As the pretty
Blonde policewoman says:
"If you don't tell me
Your name and phone number—
I'll make a live specimen
Of you, and you
Will be as sad
As I am," as she beat

Her chest and dangled
Her tongue, then wet
Each lip like a wolf.
When her father came
To pick her up
He grimaced at her
As she walks solitary
Under his wing
Covered over by his blue
Striped suit.

She is alone, but wise at last.

**By Lisa Rhodes**

## Warmonger

To observe an entire culture—
Transform into blazing ruins:
Buildings, which had taken years to erect—
Demolished within minutes,
By the machines of destruction and doom.
This can put a smile on the face of any individual
Such as myself.

The sound of metal shells colliding as they
      Reach the target—
Gives me an orgasmic high,
And I laugh as brawny, storm troopers attack
and     ravish
Those infirmed, fearful weaklings.

Human life
Serves only two functions:
Domination and annihilation.


**By Greg Roman**

# P.B. Performance Piece

Playing Baseball in the park
can be a favorite colored-folk pastime.
Bats, balls, good times all summer long,
and "what'd we do, officer?"
We're a mess of Black and White
some Red and Blue
We put our bats down
to save, now Black and Blue,
Brother Tim.
But some, not us, whipped out their bats,
and with divine pleasure,
beat and beat and beat down
on gray concrete
spilled more Red blood
as oxygen, not hit, Blue blood
sprayed an array of more can paint
He fainted
        Cold knocked out.
Face pulled apart
where there were no seams.
This team took no prisoners,
Listeners heard the screams
and saw in the beams of light
the primary colors of
Red, Blue, Black and White
But no fight was put up,
They shut up.
As they saw Alicia and Rodney and
Poor lil' Abner
Get their bodies massacred.
It occurred to be a helpless situation
Of tribulation.
Scared adults
Protect themselves
From "Peace" officers.

"And what'd she do, officer?
Did she pick a fight with you?"

Fists, knives- she didn't have either one
But look at the terror of sticks n' guns
Didn't yo mama tell you 'bout hittin' women?
Oh, I git it, ya'll think you're superhuman or somethin'
The badge gotcha feelin' hign n' mighty
But frightening is what you be to me.
Mr. Po got me feelin' the pound
That sick sound
Of stick on skin
To the fin
You don't git your fill
Until
That build
Is limp and lifeless."
"Try this,"
You tell your homies
to get in on the action,
"C'mon and join me
In a game of
Pin the tail on the Concrete."

"A power trip that'll give you a high,
make you feel like God.
so, in your name,
what'd we do to deserve this?
Pay our taxes on time
so you can have a fine time
playing Russian roulette
With a life,
that's not yours?
You sport your gear
so we fear you
rather than need you
at our parties of communal vibin'
you're tryin' to find your way
through mobs of homies
to pick your prey wisely.
Kindly officer,
could you stop harrassin' me?
Killin' me softly…
I'm sadly taking this abuse

I have no use
For <u>your</u> wiggity wack role
In right - winged agenda
I send a letter to the Gates
And no judgment is given…
I'm livin in a fucked up world,
and the twirl of your baton
drowns me in a swirl of blood on
curbside - Quick!
Hide at home
I'm all alone
with the pigs bangin' on my door,
and they're not here to see if I'm alright.
"Peace, officer, peace"
To Protect and To Serve
                                    Na
To destruct and to Pervert.
We know about up-the-ass down-the-throat
We know about video-tape advantage
We know what goes on, on that Riverside
So,
"Peace, officer, Peace"


**By D'Lo**

# Black And Proud Women In Spite Of Prison

*(Dedicated to the women at Westchester Women's Correctional Facility)*

I

Here we are black women
sitting in a prison, our children
are home, waiting alone with
no place to grow.
Why are we slaves locking up our time?
We should be out there thriving, instead of dying.

II

We should be living out there instead of dying—
not babies birthing babies: fallen women.
Our ancestors were proud slaves working hard times
who fought injustice for us and for the future children.
Singing a slaves hymns, no one is alone.
The slave train stops on time!

III

We need to respect ourselves, we're not alone.
Bring the children's voices away from the dying.
Educate them until they're grown.
Americas future is born inside the woman.
Her seeds will produce bright children.
Wave your strong arms free time after time.

IV

Always keep records of your dreams for good times.
Share your joy with Him when alone.
Prepare your mind for the inquisitive child—
Guide them in this life and resurrect the mind dying.
Be black and proud, you were born a woman;
Reach your powers like the sun so you can grow.

V

Born to win, good goals always grow.
Learning to read and write may take some time—
Your a double minority: black and a woman.
Spend your time well when alone.

Teach important lessons to your children.
Attend to the living will before your dying.


**By Lisa Rhodes**

## On Rodney King*

I,

Felt the whumps on Rodney King

And fell

As Earth began to swing

My cheeks volcanoled with crimson blood

Head ached and rang

From thud to thud

I scrambled, scrambled

To my feet

To march towards a distant beat

But convulsed

Again

And spun around

As White guardians

Drove me

Deep

Into the ground.

**By. Ira E. Harrison**

*Dedicated to this 25 year old Black Man's March 3, 1991, police brutality beating by four White uniformed Los Angeles policemen and the 81 second video recording of this event, and written after having been taken to the spot by two sons.

# TO AMADOU DIALLO

Caught in the act

Of being law and order-ly

You

Triggered an act

Of being slaughtered-ly

By those oathed

"To protect and To serve,"

While reaching for your wallet

Were served

41 rounds of ammo

Citizen Amadou Diallo,

Fired from NYPD's finest—

19 hitting the mark—

Exploding the well worn spark among us

"Where Oh Where in America is Justice?"

**By Ira E. Harrison**

## Ready Fire

Black and Puerto - Rican men
stand in front of the prison firing squad
swathed in white cloth garments,
feet bound into chains, hooking
the livelihood of their families.

Hair parted on the side slick
from perspiration—
dashes the executioner's hands.

Women have marched to the front line
holding babies in their arms
with their legs exposed, lips bare.
This is their last plea for their husband's innocence.

Any tears falling from their husband's somber eyes
cast shadows of the next
generations revenge.


**By Lisa Rhodes**

# Bloody Beatings

Bloody beatings

With billy clubs, steel pipes and fists…

Heads bashed…stomachs kicked…

What rights does a murderer, rapist or junkie have?

A knife is given to a killer

To scare off a witness for the Major.


Escape


He slashed his arm, cut an artery,

But he's diagnosed "paranoid schizophrenic"

A mental case from Vietnam.


His nose was broken in the county jail…

He killed a policeman

No surgery while on death row

Let him breathe with difficulty till he's killed.

**By Billy B. Barrett**

## In Memory Of Eleanor Bumpurs

*(Killed in 1984 by Police Gunfire)*


What cold wind rattled
the window of an old
Harlem Apartment, knocking
over twelve yellow stemmed roses
floating across her kitchen floor,
thorns jutting out like numerous razor blades
when she reaches down
to pick them up—
cutting open her pained flesh,
so drops of blood sprinkle boldly on the floor
from her index finger.

Something might change, she thought—
an apartment might spring up.
She prayed for a miracle,
an end to eviction notices,
an end to her nightmare.

A knock banged across
her front door.  It was 2 policemen
and a supervising officer
with large plexiglas shields,
a shotgun, restraining hook
and service revolvers
harassing her about when
she was planning to move—
an attempt to evict her
for being $96.85 lapsed
in her rent.  Her blood pressure jumped
even higher, the pump
of her heart frantically
pounded her chest, bubububump…
bubububump…bubububump.
It felt like a heart attack
was coming on,
and she then heard the whelps and squeals of her

door being pried open.
She rushed for her kitchen
knife, scared to death,
suddenly the door flung open
and there was a shot that
took off most of her hand
that held the knife, then she was shot again.
Sixty-seven year old, 270 lb.
arthritic, Eleanor Bumpurs lay
dead on the floor.  Killed
by the Police.

Couldn't this have been
your grandma? Or my grandma?
But not someone whites' grandma,
nobody would dare manhandle, yet scare
someone whites' arthritic, 270 lb. grandma
with a restraining hook, large plexiglas shields,
shotgun and service revolvers for a $96.85 rent check.

Isn't this how it happened? Do you remember?
I couldn't find any information, today in 2001
about the incident in The New York Times which
barely said a word then, now, and probably will say
nothing about anything for the next decade or so.


**By Lisa Rhodes**

## Mike The Knife

*(Dedicated to those who lost their lives by the reckless drunks in police uniforms)*

Two hitchhikers jumped into a car, the driver flicked his knife,
six inches.  "Next time you think about hitchhiking..." Betty groped
the right door handle hard, her friend Penny pushed her, "I'll teach you both a
lesson..." fiercely
shaking his arm, jabbing a hole through a 50 pound bag of salt.
The winter wind howled, the door swung open sweeping salt into his eye.
Penny and Betty rolled out of the car bouncing like oranges

peeling their way across an empty lot in Queens, New York angrier then rotten
oranges
where the Police ride around drunk Saturday nights collecting knives,
guns, chains, sticks and junk, chewing on packs of gum fiercely while
watching a solicitous women in a white fur coat being groped
by a drug dealer in the back car seat of a blue 1963 Chevy, licking saliva salts—
over her protesting no's.  She pounded his back piercing

her screams above the police sirens bleating pulse, drowning the fierce
policeman shouting obscenities, his stick waving like a torch, electric neon
orange
drugstore advertisements flashed like a lip synched message: Try Epson salt
baths for relief from cuts, bruises... it cleans better then astringent... good for
cuts from knife...
as the policeman stumbled on a rock, falling on his knees, groping
for his handcuffs that slipped under the car before his eyes,

blurred red after rubbing his fingers into his swelled watering eyes
downcast in the shadows of his partners bright light fiercely
searching the ground powdered white.  He dizzily grovels
on his knees grounding down cigarette butts, cinders flicking orange
burnt a hole in his pants glistening in blood from a pen knifed
into his knee as he fumbled for his ticket book licking his salty

fingers one by one, ripping pages into shreds, bits falling like salt
dotting over the colorful graffitied ground with bold letters spelling,
For wide-eyed susans, please call Mike the Knife.
The policeman got up with his teeth clenching a stupid grin coerced
across his cheeks rounded with porous skin thick and turning orange

in embarrassment from the smell of his clothes groping over his large beer belly.

**By Lisa Rhodes**

## I Was There

In memory of Larry, may justice prevail,

for the night he was killed in the county jail.

I'm writing for the future, because of the past,

knowing what I say, may be my last.

But, write I must, out of great despair,

in hopes that someone will listen and care.

Just what will it take to make people see,

their children are dying so needlessly?

Merciless Killings, by bands of men,

protected by badges of silver and tin.

Now, as I sit here upon my bed,

wondering who will be next dead?

Will it be me, for writing this?

They'll say it was suicide, and nothing amiss.

This is the way it will probably go,

as their evidence will surely show.

I was quite insane; out of my head,

Jumped head - first off my bed.

But, before this happens, I want to say;

"Don't believe it, it never happened that way!

And neither was it an accident,

the night Larry was beaten till his life was spent.

You might think this nonsense, but please beware,

I know what happened that night,

I was there!

**By Billy B. Barrett**

# The men move like men move through a dream

Move like men move through heavy air, a liquid
        atmosphere.
It is midnight in the projects, in the dead-end
      neighborhoods where
Worn-down Negroes move through the street,
       contemplative and wary.
Footfall on snow is gravel shaken in a colander
      with no figure
Coincident with the sound.
In this subaqual landscape where seadrift molts
      to snowdrift
A single car circles the block.  It is a bathysphere
      submerged
In this night's dark ocean and it is at the end
      of its lifeline
Where oxygen turns solid and creatures,
Evolved beyond eyes, see through their skins,
And their inverted hearts pump upward.
The car boxes the block once again and parks
      midway between the traffic-light and the ambulance.
EMS steady themselves on the seafloor ice, cross the
      littered porch into the cold hall.
The ambulance light whips through a distracted systole
      and diastole.
The windows covered in curtains and newspapers glow blood,
      then gone, with each rotation.
The snow in moonlight alternately glows
      like a hemorrhage on cotton.
Then gone.  Through the door can be seen a frieze of faces
      that peer along the banister-rail,
Faces hooked by curiosity and panic,
Faces of fish that live in caves and venture out
When tragedy or the unfamiliar draws the outer world down
And in.  The engine disengages.  The still car waits in the street
      blocked by the ambulance with its rear doors
Swung open, empty, its low inner light, tanks, blankets folded
      and stacked, stretcher.  Likewise the cruisers on the corner,
Each faces the other, each empty, dashboard and warning lights.

The traffic signal next block distant goes yellow, then
    red, green, yellow, then red, then green, yellow.  Another
    stretcher
Thrown on the snowbank, angled upward and held in this
    foreboding tableau in which
Nothing happens.  The windows mist.
The front door opens.  Two cops exit.  One cop sticks
His report book in his pocket.  The other cop shifts
His holster belt.  The two sit
In one cruiser.  The beacon light goes yellow, then red, then
    green, yellow, then red.  The gray exhaust follows the white snow,
    rises as slowly as the light changes.  The cruiser door slams.
    it is a distant
Sudden charge detonated.  The front cruiser leaves. The rear cruiser
    tacks against the bank,
Deep tread catches snow, pulls away.  The wipers on the parked car
    clear a crescent, cease. The scene goes inclementally
    pointillist.  Two EMS
Leave the house, wait in the ambulance.  The parked car starts,
    idles, considers, pulls without sound next to the ambulance.
    Its window
Lowers. Breath rises from the inside dark against the dashlight.
—Overdose.—Overdose.—Who is it.—Who knows.—Is it
    Yogi on the third floor who trucks out of Brooklyn by way of
    Totowa or his wife
    Marilynn who cadges Heineken and affection in the local spots
        or their elder son
    Jonathan who draws pictures with the caveat: "But, Mom, I don't
        always paint what you see" or their younger son
    Terry who writes poems with the self possession of an old man
    who ruminates on baseball.—
                —No.
                  Some colored girl on
    the first floor.— Dead.—Almost.— Stacy.—That's her
    name.  How come.— No reason.—
The ambulance attendant turns back to the dispatch radio.  The car
    window
Closes.  The gone car stops at the light one block distant, its
    signal flashes red flashes red, then turns.  Low reefs of plowed
    snow obscure both curbs.  Grillwork and wheels protrude
    like fossils.  The car motors between, under streetlight,
    stops at the next light.  A woman darts

To the window.  She smiles and beckons, her mouth forms words, she
        angles towards the passenger-door.  The light
And the air around go green.  The car pulls away.  The woman floats
        for a second in the street then flees beyond the ice-drift.


God forgive our sacred hearts.


**By Robert Gardner**

# It Doesn't Really Matter

It doesn't really matter
if you are a rapist, robber,
or murderer.
Whom ever you are, belong to—
or are a relative to who is this or that;
We the poets will destroy you
in articulate ways by
verb and noun, adjective—
and adverb;
until you are dead.


**by Annonymous**

## For Tyisha Miller

When can the sun pull its'
hood over our heads
and disguise us as Apollo
to radiate in justice
like the tiers of a step ladder
so we can balance injustice
in the palm oil burning
in our hands?

How do four white policemen
walk away after shooting
a 19 year old black woman
a total of 27 times?
Four times in the head, shattering
her skull, then her chest—
and the rest riveted her demeanor
like a tin can for target practice.

Tyisha is a victim like
many of us could be
who depend on the police
to help us in times of
crisis only to find ourselves
being treated as a criminal,
an animal with no feelings.

What was her crime?
Being black, female—
a double minority,
having a flat tire,
being physically sick
and unconscious,
scared with a gun in her lap,
living in a violent neighborhood,
never realizing that the ultra right white police,
are ignorant, cold, frightened fags, scared
of their own shadow in the face
of a black persons eyes,

cowards, quick to use force
and their hate to solve every
situation dealing with blacks,
killers not protectors
with every given opportunity
to eradicate the black race.

As history as shown us
with the killings of
Arthur Miller, Marian Johnson,
Elizabeth Mangum, Peter Funches,
Jay Parker, Michael Stewart,
Eleanor Bumpurs, Nicholas Bartlett,
Yvonne Smallwood, Stephen Kelly,
Kevin Thorpe, Phillip Parnell,
Patrick Dorismond, Amadou Diallo
and many many others, black
people are an endangered species
of human life who need never
rely on the police except when
they are suicidal and in need of
a viable hand to help end their life.
This is the sad state of the American Justice System.

When will black brothers and sisters join hands
and realize that we must stick together as a cause,
and not be the effect of death threats, racism, and fear?
Because if we don't, we will die like the American Indian,
in a cloud of dust piled on heaps of ash and pain.

**by Lisa Rhodes**

## For Patrick Dorismond

All your life, you wait
and wait to forget the one
time run in with the police
as a juvenile, an incident
that got thrown out of court
and no record was ever made
of it.  Forever sealed, hidden,
covered over with dust.
At, 21 the golden
number on your license
said you're an adult,
a free man; you rejoiced
in your strength and were healed.

Now, years later married with kids,
your still treated like a punk,
stopped on the street by
undercover cops asking
you if you know where
to cop drugs, harassing you,
wanting you, to feel their needs:
to succeed against every black man
they see, to target a grudge,
expose their hate at you
for not taking their bait,
they can't wait to infuriate
then strike you dead.

That's all it takes, them
and their white skin,
to justify every derogatory
action they engage in, their
inflated egos bursting like junkies
on a Heroin high, they know
with their White Skin they'll
get by in every court in America,
with every uncle tom freak,
unable to speak with their black

skin scrubbed white inside
their pathetic dumb ass mind.

There's a way other White bigots
will close their eyes and say
just another nigger was killed
today.  But let me tell you
there won't be another day,
for the great white hope,
to park his car on top of me,
because I'm a woman of many
colors you see, but at my core—
I'm the blackest bitch and you'll never forget
the day you lay your mouth, hand,
and farts allover me.  I'm watching
you watching me and it sure stinks
from the foul odor of your perspiration
as I gasp for air so I can finally breathe.


**By Lisa Rhodes**

## For Shane Daniels

Long Island still bites
like knats from the memory
of that nightmarish evening when
Shane Daniels was mercilessly
beaten by two white off duty police
officers, high after toasting glasses
of good old boys champagne—
using a car safety club
attempted to kill, and
instead gouged a large deep hole
into Shane's head, putting him in
a coma so he would awake
with no memory of them or
what happened to him, on
that night, out with his white
girlfriend, he a handsome
light skinned black man,
fit to be a movie star—
innocently awakened their racist rage
and jealousy.  Imagine a black man with
one of <u>THEIR</u> women, a woman
that wouldn't waste her time
with the likes of them: riff raff,
respectless wife beaters, faceless,
dishonoring, pathetic, emasculated
garbage talking, filthy parasites
living off the AMERICAN TAX PAYERS
bank rolls to bruise the human race
beyond red to the fragile skeleton frame
of humanity.  What should their penalty
be?

**By Lisa Rhodes**

*Ann McCall*

# The ghetto stomp

Hate fuels a tango into the night.

The veil from another's eye drapes over my shoulders.

Shrieks of terror coat the block as their eyes noose an innocent heart into the grave.

The misty swirl of night lathers the gavel through corridors lined in the ghetto.

My heart thumps to the maestro's barren serenade, as he stalks a prize.


Flashlight sears terror over my skin.

I pray the warrior hunts another shadow through the night.


Coyness costumes his bloody passion that rewards bureaucracy.

Fake sincerity seeps through caked armor.

Feigned smiles snarl a wicked bite.


False stares examine the fearful herd for a plump runt to skewer.

Luscious batons dangle death from hooked leather.


Shriek from steel beating bones rives the scabs of previous meals.

The frenzied soldiers swing nets overheads.

Screaming maggots devour life.

Prey run to nowhere.

Each stomp bruises blossom rings around my shattered hearts.

The sprint to Heaven chills a cold dinner, for the future.

The leap to prison stuns the sea hollow pigs that beg for darker blood.

Each night misery pushes us deeper into the ghetto quiet room.


Many masks revolve around coffins.

None witness truth.

All spirits wash into the Abyss.

No water rinses away screams.


**By Monk**

*Ann McCall*

# Heavy Recognition


I STAND AMONGST THE MOST HONORABLE HUSBANDS AND
COMMITTED WIVES—
WHO THRIVE ON LIVING AND DYING FOR SOMETHING MUCH
GREATER THAN THEMSELVES
CELEBRATING <u>STILL</u>—
IN THE MIDST, OF CONFLICTUAL DAILY RITUALS
OUR SPIRITUAL RAINDANCE REMAINS CRITICAL TO REASONING
SO DECIPHER OUR MOVEMENTS - WHILE OUR RHYTHM OF SPEECH
OUT HUSTLES MISEDUCATION
RENDERING IT'S AIM TO TRAIN US USELESS

WE STAND AROUND THE FIRE OF DESIRE AND HOPE - CLUTCHIN'
FLAMES
NAMING CHILDREN NAMES THAT FEAR NOT DEATH
OUR DEPTH IS PROVEN BY CHARACTER - "NO SPEECHES"
WE SIMPLY LET OUR ACTIONS BRING IDEAS TO LIFE—
BRIGHT ENOUGH TO INSPIRE SINGLE MOTHERS UNWANTED FOR
THE RIGHT REASONS
AND BLACK MALES SHACKLED UP FOR MANY SEASONS
DISAPPEARING DADS - DEAD
WE MAKE EM' REAPPEAR RESPONSIBLE, TO BALANCE
RELATIONSHIPS NON ILLOGICAL
THE DAMAGE IS PSYCHOLOGICAL AND OBSTACLES LIKE BILLS,
LOVE, AND DEATHTOLLS
WEAR HOLES - IN OUR INTERIOR

<u>STILL</u>...
INFERIOR DOESN'T REGISTER -  WE KEEP IT MOVING
IN AND OUT OF SECLUSION - NOT WAITING ON SOME LEADER TO
EMERGE
AND GIVE "<u>THE WORD</u>"...
CORN BRAIDED CROWN KINGS AND QUEENS FORM HOLY UNIONS
INTERLOCKING ETERNITY WITH FUSION—
BUILDING THE MOST HONORABLE FAMILIES EVEN OUT OF <u>GHETTO
DEBRIS</u>
WHERE BROKEN PROMISES AND DREAMS BLOW OUT IN THE
STREET LIKE LITTER

WE'RE MADE TO MASTER EMOTIONS AND SEEK KNOWLEDGE LIKE BREATHING—
SEARCHING DEEP WITHIN OURSELVES TO FIND WHAT ANCESTORS LEFT—
FROM PERCEPTION TO CONCEPTION - FROM WHAT YOU SEE TO WHAT YOU THINK—
WERE DIVINE BY NATURAL INSTINCT - NOT SINNERS BY INSTINCT AND THATS HEAVY RECOGNITION…
LIKE REALIZING THAT IT'S you in my DESCRIPTION


**By Amen Kush (Demond Jones) THE FIELD HAND MOVEMENT**

# The Search

I stand at street corners
rumagin through waste baskets.
Clad in tattered garments, soul and body now exposed
searching feverishly for a find that will fit into
the jigsaw of my broken life.

A bit of colored glass, a bottle cap, yesterday's news
memories pour forth, a bottle cap, yesterday's news
memories pour forth, fragmented, unrelated, echoing
pain and joy.
Yet the pieces do not fit, so that I may know
who I am, and why and of my lost forgotten past.

My search continues, across the street, into the waste.
I am not unmindful of the passerbys
who stare in disbelief at me and my activity.
Cold eyes betray their angry scorn.
Can it be? I am a threat to the standards they have set.

My shopping bag is full, full of precious jewels.
They are found in the most unlikely places, if we dare to look.
I return home to my dingy room.
It is very cold, so I light the stove
and then proceed to work on the jigsaw of my life
spread across the bed.

Perhaps this will fit, no, or this
bit of glass, yes
memories pour forth connected, I am whole, no longer lost,
the jigsaw is complete.

Tomorrow I will return to the street corners
once more, to return my find to their home beneath the waste.
They were only lent to me like in search of a pad.
I need search no more.
My life begins anew.

**By Rosemarie Rhodes**

# AUTHORS BIOGRAPHIES

**ISRAEL BAYER**: He has worked with numerous groups on social justice issue's in Portland, Oregon and in Denver. Mr. Bayer was submission's editor for a year with Copwatch and street roots, a street newspaper in Portland. His poems first appeared in a low-budget chapbook called "Working Class Revolt."

**BILLY BROOKS BARRETT**: Poet planning on publishing his own book of poetry.

**ROBERT BETTS**: His poetry has appeared in college literary journals in the Boston area, in Curbstone and in anthologies. Mr. Betts has three poems due to be published in 2001 by the editor of HazMat. He recommends reading White Lies, by Jessie Daniels, ISBN# 0415912903.

**MICHAEL CASEY**: His first book Obscenities was in the Yale Younger Poet Series in 1972. The reprint is now planned by Gerald Costanzo at the Carnegie-Mellon University Press. Recently a second book was published Millrat with two printings from Adastra Press. His third book, The Million Dollar Hole, named after an engineer excavation pit at Fort Leonard Wood, Missouri, has been accepted by Orchises Press of Alexandra, Virginia for a January 2001 publication date. Mr. Casey's writing has appeared in three anthologies: The Yale Younger Poet Anthology, edited by George Bradley; The Vietnam Reader, edited by Stewart O'Nan; and From Both Sides Now, edited by Philip Mahony.

**CYNTHIA CAVANAUGH**: Cynthia A. Cavanaugh works as a college composition instructor. She received a B.A. from the Universities of South Florida and a J.D. from Stetson University College of Law.

**DEVORIE FRANZWA**: Poet living in California.

**ROBERT GARDNER**: Poet living in New Jersey.

**JOSÉ GOUVEIA**: Hyannis Port poet presently writing a biography on Grace Gouveia Collinson. He is not related to Grace Gouveia. He appeared in the 1999 National Poetry Slam, Chicago, Illinois.

**SAM FRIEDMAN**: Sam Friedman is a socialist, AIDS researcher, and poet. He has previously published about 70 poems in magazines and journals including Lips, Long Shot, Canadian Dimension, journal of Progressive Human Services, and Home Planet News. His first book of poetry is Needles, drugs, and defiance:

Poems to organize by.  He is also the author of Teamster Rank and File (Columbia University Press, 1982) and of Social Networks, Drug Injectors' Lives, and HIV/AIDS. (Friedman SR, Curtis R, Neaigus A, Jose B, Des Jarlais DC. 1999. New York Kluwer/ Plenum.)

**IRA HARRISON**: A graduate from Syracuse Central High School in 1951.  He graduated from Moorehouse College, Atlanta, Ga.  with a BA in Sociology in 1955; won a scholarship to Atlanta University in 58, finishing his MA in sociology and anthropology in 1959.  Taught a year in rural Georgia, and entered Syracuse University the summer of 1960.  He was awarded the Ph. D. in Social Sciences (Sociology, Anthropology, Metropolitan Studies) in 1967, from the Maxwell School of Citizenship and Public Affairs.  From 1963 to 1967, he worked as a researcher and church planner with the Ohio Council of Churches, and the Southwestern Ohio Regional Church Planning Board conducting studies in Youngstown, Lordstown, Canton, and Dayton, Ohio.  From 1967 to 1972, he worked as a public Health Behavioral Scientist with the Department of Health, the Commonwealth of Pennsylvania; researching migrant farm workers, and helping low income people get OEO neighborhood health centers in Harrisburg and York.  He earned a Masters of Public Health, John Hopkins University, Baltimore, Md. in 1971, and returned to the Department of Health as Director of the Division of Behavioral Science.  He has researched traditional healers in Nigeria and Botswana.  In 1974, he was recruited to the Department of Anthropology, at the University of Tennessee in Knoxville, and retired as an emeritus professor in 1998.  Currently he is a Coordinator of 21st Century Racial Justice Program, Moorehouse College Research Institute, Moorehouse College, Atlanta, Georgia, his alma mater.  He has authored, co-authored and/or book reviews on anthropology, public health, and church planning, and three books of poetry.  He is married to Claire Crooks Harrison, and has three children: Meri-Louise, Ira Michael, and Timothy Scott by a previous marriage.  He has a 16 year old grandson named Marcus.  He has authored, co-authored and/or book reviews on anthropology, public health, and church planning, and three books of poetry.

**JON HILLSON**: Poet living in California.

**CHRISTINA K.  HUTCHINS**: She currently teaches process philosophy and lesbian/gay theory at the Pacific School of Religion in Berkeley and is completing an interdisciplinary Ph.D. in philosophy of religion, gender/sexuality studies and poetry at the Graduate Theological Union in Berkeley. Her poems have recently appeared in Nimrod, Cream City Review, Fireweed, Thelma, Iris, Alligator Juniper, Portland Review, Southern Poetry Review, Bay Windows, Byline, Paterson Literary Review, Harvard Gay and Lesbian Review, Poetry Motel, Ruah, Frogpond, Cicada, American Tanka, and in various anthologies. In addition to a chapbook and compact disc, Collecting Light (Berkeley: Acacia Books, 1999), Ms. Hutchins is finishing a full length poetry collection, Music of Found Summers in which her poem "Between Here and There," first appeared. She was named a finalist for the 1997 Allen Ginsberg Prize, the 1977 Billee Murray Denny Award, and the 1999 Pablo Neruda Prize and won the 1997 Haiku Society's Senryu Award and the 1997-98 Villa Montalvo Biennial Poetry Prize. Her writing is currently supported in part by the Money For Women/Barbara Deming Memorial Fund and the Uncommon Legacy Foundation for lesbian advocacy.

**DAVID G. KATZ**: He is a graduate of the University of Hartford. He is single, lives in New York and is an Associate Editor for Blender Magazine. He has no hate for the police, just brutality.

**AMEN KUSH(DEMOND JONES)**:A Poet and member of THE FIELD HAND MOVEMENT.

**J. KEIKO LANE**: J. Keiko Lane is the fourth generation Japanese American Daughter of an artist and a jazz musician. A long term survivor of ACT UP and Queer Nation, she spent her youth organizing in the grassroots AIDS, queer, and solidarity movements in Los Angeles. Her poetry and essays have appeared in Calyx: A Journal of Art and Literature by Women, Infected Faggot Perspectives, Americas Review, Sex and Single Girls, and the Journal of the Nuclear Age Peace Foundation, which awarded her the 1998 Barbara Mandigo Kelly Peace Poetry Award. She has recently completed a manuscript of poems called The Rememberers. She lives in Northern California, where she writes and studies Somatic Psychology.

**SABASTIAN LAZER**: "i was born in transylvania.
my soul rides on two blue horses, my eyes,
my heart is brave like my middle name, Decebal,
and i intend to die on earth."

**JEFF MANN**: Jeff Mann grew up in southwest Virginia and southern West Virginia, receiving degrees in English and forestry from West Virginia University. He has published in The Laurel Review, Antietam Review, Poet Lore, Appalachian Heritage, The Hampden-Sydney Poetry Review, Spoon River Poetry Review and Prairie Schooner. His collection Bliss won the 1997 Stonewall Chapbook Competition and was published in 1998 by Brick House Books. Fireflies Mountain, which won the 1999 Poetic Matrix Chapbook Competition, was published in 2000. He teaches Appalachian Studies and creative writing at Virginia Tech.

**MONK**: A Poet.

**FELICIA MORGENSTERN:** A globe-trotting teacher/writer/poet, teaches English and creative writing to newly-arrived immigrants in the Baltimore-Washington Area. She frequently performs her poetry and prose at literary benefits, art galleries, museums, poetry festivals, universities and book stores. Felicia was recently featured on television and in a spoken word cd. She is the author of the night mother earth told father sky she was tired of the missionary position.

**SHERYL L. NELMS**: I'm from Marysville, Kansas. I graduated from South Dakota State University, with a B.S. iv Family Relations and Child Development.

I've had over 4,500 poems, articles and short stories published. Some of the magazines, anthologies and textbooks that have used my work are: READER'S DIGEST, MODERN MATURITY, KALEIDOSCOPE, CAPPER'S, GRIT, COUNTRY WOMAN, POETRY NOW, CONFRONTATION, Strings, This Delicious Day, The American Anthology, and Men Freeing Men.'

Eight collections of my poetry have been published: Their Combs Turn Red in the spring, The Oketo Yahoos, Strawberries and Rhuharb, Rural America, Land of the Blue Paloverde, Friday Night Desperate and a chapbook. My eight book, Aunt Emma Collected Teeth was recently released by Sweet Annie Press.

**EWUARE OSAYANDE:** (talkingdrum@hotmail.com) is a poet, cultural analyst and political activist. He is the author of several books including So the Spoken Word Won't be Broken: The Politics of the New Black Poetry and the forthcoming book of poems, Caught at the Crossroads Without a Map from Undaground RR X-Press.

**LINDA G. PELTZ, Ph.D.**: Dr. Linda Peltz is a Psychologist and Psychoanalyst in private practice in Hicksville, New York. She also has a grant from Chase Bank to teach 6th graders about their feelings through literature discussions.

**LISA RHODES**: A graduate from Sarah Lawrence College in Bronxville, N.Y. where she received a MFA in poetry in 1999. She has been published in AIM, Journal of Poetry Therapy, Poetry Motel, Poetry FORUM, Left Jab, Footsteps, and in numerous anthologies. She teaches poetry part-time at Westchester Community College through Continuing Education and has mentored prisoners in creative writing through Pen America's Prison Writing Program. She has worked as a substitute teacher for Rockland County Public Schools. Additionally, she is a freelance writer and working on a series of children's books and publishing her own book of poems.  She is a veteran of the United States Army and a member of Toastmasters International.  She has volunteered at Helen Hayes Hospital, Nyack Hospital, Rockland State Psychiatric Center and given numerous poetry readings at bookstores and libraries, and cafes. She is single and living in New York.

**ROSEMARIE RHODES**: She graduated Bellevue Nursing School with a RN degree and graduated Hunter College with a B.A. in English.

**GREG ROMAN**: My name is Greg Roman.  I was born on July 2nd, 1967 in the state of New York.  I have lived in Rockland County, in the village of Pomona, for 34 years.  I'm an Assistant Teacher at the Tops For Tots Children's Center in Spring Valley, N.Y. for 9 years going on 10.  I'm a Senior at St. Thomas Aquinas College in Sparkill, N.Y.  I have been writing poems for about 7 or 8 years, and writing fiction stories for the past twelve years.

**STEVEN M. SLOAN**: Professor Steven M. Sloan is a scholar, teacher, and poet who has been widely anthologized, as well as widely published in poetry magazines, journals, and newspapers.  He is a graduate of the University of Wisconsin - Whitewater (where he was a member of the Editorial Board for its poetry publication: The Muse), and is also a graduate of the University of Wisconsin - Madison.  He is the author of multiple books or pamphlets and remains committed to the art.  The editor of Columbia Publications has said of him that he is, "a talented poet" whose work, "touches upon many topics and emotions," and that, "his imagery is characteristically spectacular, as well as thought-evoking (Lana M. Wegend, Editor)."  Dana Minor, Editor of the poetry journal: Sublime Odyssey, has said that, "Sloan has a definite capacity for ringing phrases."  He is currently living in Kenosha, Wisconsin.

# ADDITIONAL INFORMATION SOURCES:

**American Civil Liberties Union**
132 West 43rd St.
New York, N.Y. 20036
212-944-9800

**American Friends Service Committee**
Immigration Law Enforcement Monitoring Project
3515 Allen Parkway
Houston, TX 77019
713-524-5428

**Commission on Accreditation for Law Enforcement Agencies (COALEA)**
4242-B Chain Bridge Road
Fairfax, VA 22030
703-352-4225

**Community United Against Violence**
514 Castro Street
San Francisco, CA 94114
415-864-3112
Lesbian/gay rights advocacy organization

**COPWATCH**
2022 Blake Street
Berkeley, CA 94704
510-548-0425

**INTERNATIONAL ASSOCIATION FOR CIVILIAN OVERSIGHT OF LAW ENFORCEMENT**
(IACOLE)
1204 Wesley Avenue
Evanston, IL 60202
312-353-4391

**National Association of Criminal Defense Lawyers**
1110 Vermont Avenue, N.W., Suite 1150
Washington, D.C. 20010
202-986-2070

**National Black Police Association (NPBA)**
3251 Mt. Pleasant St. N.W.
Washington, D.C. 20010
202-986-2070
*Brochures on how to handle encounters with police, entitled "What to do when stopped by police."

**National Coalition For Police Accountability (NCPA)**
59 E. Van Buren, Suite 2418
Chicago, IL 60603
312-663-5392

**Police Foundation**
1001 22nd St., N.W., Suite 200
Washington, D.C. 20037
202-833-1460

**Police Watch**
611 S. Catalina, Suite 409
Los Angeles, CA 90005
213-387-3325

Model legal referral programs for victims of police abuse.  Some training for police abuse litigators.  Data base on incidents of abuse in Southern California.

**Police Executive Research Forum (PERF)**
2300 M Street, N.W.
Washington, D.C. 20037
202-833-1460

Non-profit consulting group, primarily engaged in research and demonstration projects on innovative police programs.  Involved in some of the most important research projects in policing since the 1970s. Professional Association of persons involved in civilian review of the police.  Membership consists primarily of staff members of local civilian review agencies. Annual meeting.  Newsletter. Periodically publishes a compendium of civilian review agencies.

**MALIK Organization**
284 James Street
New Haven, CT 06513
203-752-1214

fax (203) 752-214
Needs Volunteers and donations to send letters calling for intervention by Justice Department to determine if Malik E. Jones' civil rights were violated to The Honorable Janet Reno, U.S. Department of Justice, Tenth St. & Constitution Ave., NW, Washington, DC 20530

**Informational Websites:**http://www.welcomehome.org/eagles/aclu-review.txt

# Resources: BIBLIOGRAPHY

**American Civil Liberties Union.**  On The Line: Police Brutality and its Remedies.  New York.  April 1991, The ACLU's response to the Rodney King beating.  Case studies and recommendations for local and federal remedies.

**ACLU of Washington**. Coalition on Government Spying: Seattle's Surveillance Ordinance. March 1980.  Describes events leading up to city's adoption of law that limits police surveillance of citizens.

**American Friends Service Committee**.  The Police Threat to Political Liberty. Philadelphia, Pennsylvania.  1979.  Comprehensive report on police spying, with separate chapters on Seattle, Los Angeles, Philadelphia, Baltimore and Jackson, Mississippi.

**Bouza, Anthony.  The Police Mystique**: An Insiders Look At Cops, Crime and the Criminal Justice System.  New York. Plenum Press. 1990.  The author, retired police chief of Minneapolis and long considered an innovative thinker, analyzes what's wrong with American policing.

# Index of Poets by Authors Last Name.

# ABOUT THE EDITOR


Social Activist and Editor.  Graduated Sarah Lawrence College, M.F.A., with a B.A. in Journalism from Mercy College.

www.ingramcontent.com/pod-product-compliance
Lightning Source LLC
Chambersburg PA
CBHW031303060726
47590CB00003B/1032